Dartmoor

By

Arthur L. Salmon

Edition : Culturea (culurea.fr), 34 Hérault
Contact : infos@culturea.fr
Impression : BOD, Norderstedt (Allemagne)
ISBN : 9791041983087
Date de publication : juillet 2023
Mise en page et maquettage : https://reedsy.com/
Cet ouvrage a été composé avec la police Bauer Bodoni

Dartmoor

Dartmoor is a fine-sounding name, and no one would wish to displace it; yet in one sense it is a misleading and inappropriate designation of the great central Devonshire moorland. The moorland is not distinctively the moor of the Dart, any more than of the Teign, the Tavy, or the Ockment; it is the cradle-land of rivers, and there is no obvious reason why the Dart should have assumed such supremacy. But there is historic fitness about the title. It is probable that the Saxons first became acquainted with Dartmoor from the fertile district known as the South Hams, watered by the beautiful reaches of the Dart from Totnes to its mouth. The wide intermediate waste that lay between the North and the South Hams was a region of mystery to them, and they associated it with this swift, sparkling stream that issued from its cleaves and bogs.

Whatever its actual population may have been, imagination would people it with spirits and demons; while it needed no imagination to supply the storms, the blinding fogs and rains, the baying wolves that haunted its recesses. They were content to retain its old Celtic name for the river, and they applied this name to the moor as well; it became the moor of the Dart. The name Dart, supposed to be akin to Darent and Derwent, is almost certainly a derivative from the Celtic dwr, water. The moorland itself is a mass of granite upheaved in pre-glacial days, weathered by countless centuries into undulating surfaces, pierced by jagged tors, and interspersed with large patches of bog and peat-mire. This is the biggest granitic area in England, the granite extending for about 225 square miles; though that which is known as Dartmoor Forest (never a forest in our accepted meaning of the word) is considerably smaller, having been much encroached upon by tillage and enclosure. There is a further protrusion of granite on the Bodmin Moors, and again as far west as Scilly; while Lundy, in the Bristol Channel, belongs almost entirely to the same formation. Beneath the mire and peat, which are the decaying deposits of vegetable matter, lies a stratum of china-clay, which is worked productively to the south of the moors, and still more largely in Cornwall. The average height of the moorland is about 1500 feet, rising in places to a little over 2000. This elevation is exceeded in Wales, in the Lake District, and in Scotland; and nowhere does Dartmoor appear actually mountainous, one reason being that the plateau from which we view its chief eminences is always well over 1000 feet above sea level, and thus a great portion of the height is not realized. But we realize it to some extent when we notice the speed of the moorland rivers; they do not linger and dally like Midland streams, they run and dash and make a perpetual music of their motion. In winter they are strong enough to make playthings of the rough lichened boulders that confront their course; and in the hottest summers they never run dry—the mother-breast of Dartmoor has always ample nourishment. Though there is a lessening in the body of the rivers, and perhaps a surface-drought of the bogs, the moors are never really parched; drovers from the Eastern counties sometimes bring their flocks hither in a summer of great heat, to feed on Dartmoor turfs when their own home-pastures would be arid. Yet the central moor is more like a desolate waste than a pasture. Its rugged turfy surface is scattered with small and large fragments of granite, sometimes "clitters" of weather-worn boulders, sometimes masses that look as though prehistoric giants had been playing at bowls. Often strange and fantastic in shape, as twilight steals on, or the weird gloom of moorland fog, they seem to become animated; they are pixies, brownies, the ghosts of old vanished peoples; wherever we gaze they start before us; prying figures seem to be hiding behind them, ill-wishing us, or eager to lure us into desolate solitudes. The wind sighs with solitary tone through the rough grasses and tussocks; at this height its evening breath is chill even in summer. Some of the stones are shattered monuments of dead men; some perhaps had a religious significance that the world has forgotten. The loneliness of the moor is often a charm, but it can become oppressive and terrible if our mood is not buoyant. In places like these the strongest mind might yield to superstition. We seem to be in a region of the primal world, where ploughshare has never passed nor kindly grain sprung forth for the nourishment of man.

But we do not come to Dartmoor for traces of the earliest man in England; for these we must go to Kent's Cavern, Torquay, or to Brixham, not to the moors. Tokens of habitation on Dartmoor only begin with Neolithic times, and are by no means continuous. At one time there must have been a thick population; but Celt and Saxon have left little trace on the moors, and the Romans none at all. Though the Celts may have conquered the Iberian tribes here, they probably neither exterminated nor entirely dispossessed them. They were content with the fringes of the wilderness, leaving the rest to the mists, the wolves, and the lingering older race. It was man of the New Stone Age who first peopled this upland, leaving remains of his hut-dwellings, his pounds, dolmens, and menhirs, his kistvaens and his cooking-holes. Numerous as the remains are still, they were once far more so; they have been broken up or carted away for road-mending, for gateposts and threshold stones, for building, for "new-take" or other walls, and for any other purpose to which granite can be applied. This central highland may have become a refuge of the later Stone-men against invaders of better equipment: all the traces of camps are on the borders, defensive against an external enemy; within is no sign of anything but peaceful pastoral occupation and tin-streaming.

Place names, of field or of farm, enable us to infer the former existence of primitive relics: wherever there is a Shilstone (shelf stone) or a Bradstone (broad stone) we may be sure there was once a dolmen or cromlech; wherever there is a Langstone or Longstone we guess at a menhir or standing-stone. These early inhabitants of the moor had advanced far from the condition of the rude cave folk; they built themselves low circular huts, generally clustered within pounds (enclosures whose chief purpose here seems to have been the protection of cattle; some of the pounds were clearly for cattle alone). At Grimspound, near Hookner Tor, are traces of twenty-four huts, enclosed in a double wall 1500 feet in circumference. The huts had low doorways, and usually platforms for domestic purposes, with hearthstones and cooking-holes. The food to be cooked was placed in the hole, sometimes in a coarse clay pot, sometimes without, together with red-hot stones from the hearth. Near Postbridge as many as fifteen pounds can be traced, while at Whit Tor are other numerous traces. Those at Grimspound evidently belong to the Bronze Age; like different periods of architecture, the Stone and Metal Ages very much overlapped.

At first the burial of these people was in dolmens, like the fine specimen at Drewsteignton; later, cremation became the fashion, and the smaller kistvaen, or stone chest, was used. The kistvaen was covered by cairns or heaps of stones, probably placed there in tribute to the dead: there are many relics of such on the moors, as in Cornwall, but they have usually been scattered or mutilated, and the contents rifled by seekers after buried treasure. The stone-circles on the moor are, of course, entirely dwarfed by Stonehenge, but when the problem of the greater is solved we shall know that of the lesser; at present we can only conjecture. The Scaur Hill circle on Gidleigh Common is a good specimen, being about ninety-two feet in diameter; near it are several stone-rows or alignments. Dartmoor is famous for these lines of standing-stones, which are generally connected with places of burial; the longest, on Staldon, starting from a circle, runs for over two miles. These, together with the single stones or menhirs, were probably intended as memorials of persons or events, and may also have been used as places of gathering; but their religious significance, if any, can have been little more than a primitive ancestor-worship. At a later period the menhirs were often converted into crosses, and as such they are common in Devon and Cornwall.

Other tokens of the early inhabitants are to be found in the signs of tin-working, but here we have to be careful in assigning dates; much tin-mining was done in the Middle Ages, and it is not always easy to distinguish between traces that date from many years before Christ and those that belong only to the fourteenth or the fifteenth century. The advance in methods of working and in mode of living was very slight, and it is quite possible to confuse a rude hut of the medieval tinners with one of prehistoric origin. We cannot positively state what period of the Bronze Age saw the dawn of tin-working on Dartmoor, but their place in the oldest folklore gives the "tinkards" a great antiquity. The metal was streamed, or washed from the beds of the moorland rivers, cast in rough ingots, and carried on pack horses to the Stannary or mintage towns, where it was stamped and taxed. Parts of the old trackways still remain, often paved; and it was for the use of the pack-horses that the characteristic clapper-bridges were constructed, like those of Dartmeet, Postbridge, and elsewhere. These bridges are quite modern when we compare them with the stone-circles and kistvaens. There was a kind of guild or early trade union between the miners of Devon and Cornwall, reminiscent of the time when both belonged to "West Wales"; and a relic of the old jurisdiction is the Stannary Court still meeting at Truro.

After the Christian era we learn little or nothing of Dartmoor till the time of the Plantagenets, though we can gather a good deal about its border towns. The wild beasts that haunted its desolate recesses brought it some repute as a hunting-ground, and it was not included in King John's act of disafforestation. We must not be led by the term Dartmoor Forest to suppose that the moors were ever covered with woodland—certainly not within historic days; for long centuries they can only have been an almost treeless waste, with patches of trees like the surviving stunted oaks of Wistman's Wood. But the borders and some of the river valleys are beautifully wooded.

It must be confessed that the rarest beauty of the moorland belongs to its fringes, around what may be called the gateways of the moor; in the interior there is the charm of broad expanse, the glorious colour of heather, ling, and gorse, and occasionally a grand desolation of mist and tempest that may almost strike dismay. A guidebook writer has spoken of Dartmoor as "the quintessence of unlovely dreariness"; and perhaps there is some justification for his words in the immediate neighbourhood of Princetown, the solitary town of the moorland proper. In size Princetown is only a village, with a population permanently increased by the presence of about a thousand convicts and their warders; and it may be feared that a majority of visitors to the place, reaching it by train from Yelverton, are drawn by a curiosity to see the prison. They are rewarded by little but a sight of the grim bare walls. Lovers of the moor have never looked with favour either at the prison or at the tortuous little railway line that climbs to it, however much this line may be admired as a feat of engineering; but we must accept the presence of the railway ungrudgingly, for it is a fine convenience for all who wish to reach the central regions of Dartmoor. The wise visitor comes to Princetown in order to get away from it as soon as possible—to get to Two Bridges, and Crockern Tor, long the open-air parliament-place of the tinners—and to find himself in a tract of lonely country perhaps more thickly studded with immemorial remains than any other in the kingdom. The prison itself is about 1500 feet above sea level; and Great Mis Tor, a mile or so to the north, is 1760 feet. It will be realized that if this and other tors rose sheer from a low-lying plain, their height would be much more appreciable. It was Tyrwhitt, Warden of the Stannaries, who suggested that a prison should be built here, to receive the prisoners of war who were crowding the seaports; and the work was begun in 1806. Tyrwhitt lived at Tor Royal, where he entertained the Prince Regent; and tradition suggests that the Prince brought his usual habits of gaiety and dissipation when he thus visited the moorland. Americans as well as Frenchmen suffered the dismal hospitality of the gaol here, as we are reminded by one of Mr. Phillpotts's novels. Of course, the new settlement was named in honour of the Regent. A few portions, such as the granite gateway with its motto Parcere Subjectis, belong to the original buildings; and the inn "The Plume of Feathers" was built by Frenchmen. A writer has spoken of Dartmoor Prison as an example of the power of moral force, as the convicts far outnumber the honest men; but it may be supposed that bolts and bars, and the firearms of the warders, have something to say in the matter. Even with these there are occasional attempts at escape or mutiny.

When the war with France came to an end the young settlement was likely to lapse into complete decay; but in 1855 it was converted into the present convict station. The problem of dealing wisely with crime has not yet been solved; and the best that can be said for Princetown is that it is undoubtedly healthy, in spite of its bitter cold in winter; and in some sort it may be regarded as a compulsory sanatorium. Whether the moral effects are as good as the physical must be left for students of punishment to decide. Whether characters are reclaimed or no, there is an effort to reclaim the moor, which is the typical stony ground of the parable; and the gradual enclosure of parts that were formerly public is a result. But at a step we can pass from present unlovely realities to the remote and traditional.

In Fox Tor Mire, which has been partially drained but has still some ugly patches of bog, we come upon the supposed tomb of Childe the Hunter, a kistvaen, while not far off is Childe's Cross. The familiar legend tells how Childe of Plymstock was hunting on Dartmoor when he was separated from his companions in a snowstorm. He killed his horse and crept into its warm carcass to keep himself from freezing, but the expedient proved of no avail, though it apparently gave him time to scribble a kind of will on a stone, to the effect that—

"Who finds and brings me to my grave

My lands at Plymstock he shall have".

Laws regarding the witnessing of wills seem to have had no operation in those days. Tidings of his death reaching Tavistock, the monks of the abbey immediately set forth to recover the body and so inherit the estate; but it seems that they were nearly forestalled by the townsmen, and it was only by the craft of the monks, who threw a hasty bridge across the Tavy, that they reached the abbey without having to contest their capture. Some say that their competitors in the race for Childe's body were the monks of Buckland, not the folk of Tavistock. Whatever we may think of the legend, it is certain that the manor of Plymstock was attached to Tavistock Abbey from the time of the Conquest to the Dissolution.

Another local tradition is that of Fitz's Well, by the Blackabrook. It is stated that Fitz of Fitzford, with his good lady, was pixy-led while crossing the moors, and could by no means find the right path. At length they came to this well, and hastened to refresh themselves. No sooner had they drunk of the water than a veil seemed removed from their eyes; they recognized where they were, and reached home in safety. Probably the well had long been esteemed holy, though no name of a saint survives in connection with it. In gratitude Fitz enclosed the spring and placed an inscribed stone above it.

Something strange is also told of the pool Classenwell, sometimes called Clakeywell or Crazywell, which is a mile or two south of Princetown. This pool is certainly more like a lake than the better-known Cranmere, which is little better than a peat bog. Its extent of water is about an acre, lying in a hollow where were formerly mine-workings. The superstitious used to assert that this dismal pond had a voice with which it announced the names of all moor folk who were about to die. Those who passed dreaded to hear the mysterious announcement, always fearing that their own names might be cried. It cannot be doubted that winds intruding to the desolate hollow might produce weird sounds from the water, especially at night; there is a mystery and solemnity about night sounds at all times, and such things have fostered many wild myths. Here, as at Cranmere, there is a legend of a doomed spirit who howls in the darkness, like the Tregeagle of Cornwall; and here also was a belief that the pool was bottomless. There is also a touch of history here: Piers Gaveston, hiding on Dartmoor during his exile from Court, is said to have consulted the oracle of Classenwell, who foretold his fate in ambiguous language which he misinterpreted. The cry of this pool reminds us of the cry of the Dart itself—its call for the human life that it demands each year—

"River of Dart, O River Dart,

Every year thou claimest a heart".

A story tells how a farm lad named Jan Coo was lured to his death by this calling of the river. It is true that when the wind blows strongly down the Dart valley a strange, strangled kind of cry comes from the gorge, which at night-time is well calculated to strike a chill to the soul of the lonely passer. But the wind on Dartmoor can do more than this; it has given us a phantom-chase like that of the Harz Mountains, and the Wish-hounds that hunt the spirits of unchristened babes across the moors.

There is a story of a farmer riding home to Chagford from Widecombe. He heard the demon huntsman pass with his yelling hounds. Perhaps the man had indulged too freely at the village inn; certainly he dared to hail the hunter and ask what sport. "Whatever the sport, you shall have your share," came back the answer; and what he imagined to be a haunch of venison was hurled into his arms. But when he reached home, and his wife brought a light, they found that the supposed game was the dead body of their own little child.

But the moor is not always desolate and haunted; its streams are not always wild dashing torrents, nor do they always trickle through black and treacherous bog. To know the moorland thoroughly we must know it in all its moods. A passing cloud or a glorious sunset can work marvellous transformations.

Two Bridges is a good spot to begin the acquaintance. A bare road runs across the open down to a gentle hollow, where it dips, passes a narrow stream, and ascends again. The slopes around are almost as smooth as if their formation was of chalk, not granite; this might be a corner of the Sussex Downs but for the jagged tors that dream in the blue haze of the horizon. Stand for a few minutes on the bridge and let the spirit of the place steal into your heart; listen to the message of the Dart as it babbles beneath the arches. Brook and nothing more it is at present. But a reverie on the roadway is liable to be disturbed by a sudden dash of dust and savour of petrol. We may be driven from the road by the invasive motor car, but there are still the footpaths and the tameless moorland. Descending to the small stretch of meadow that borders the stream above the bridge, in a few moments we seem far removed from disconcerting evidences of a civilization that is always in a hurry.

We are by the side of a free moorland water, gliding and gurgling and whispering through a valley-bed of rugged and weeded crags, with trees that make a chequered network of the sunlight. It is a paradise of coolness and peace, where there are mossy boulders on which we can rest, or couches of fern and turf on which we can lie. The constant yet changeful music of the waters is in our ears; our eyes are soothed by the sweet umbrage of the branches, conveying the light with an alchemy that transmutes it into a green-tinged wine. Sometimes the water takes an amber tint, coloured by the fragments of rock that in almost any part form stepping-stones from side to side. In winter no such passage would be easy; the brook becomes an angry torrent, leaping with foam and impetuous fury down the rock-strewn gorge: but that which at times can become a relentless giant, at other times is like a playful nursling; the child prattles where sometimes the Titan thunders. There are miniature cascades and tiny waterfalls; the stones that are nothing to the swollen winter stream now cause its baby current to swerve and deviate, seeking for fissures that permit its flowing. It is delightful to lave one's feet in the clear tide, but the weeded stones are slippery and the bed of the stream is rough; this is no quiet sandy brooklet that children may wade in. It does not dally, but flows with a swift current of life. Many of our typical English streams are almost or quite voiceless in their course; we have to bend our heads to catch the low monotone of their flowing. But here is no pastoral brook meandering through meadowy lowlands; it runs with a gush and a tinkle; even in hot days, when the current is slender, there is always spirit and vigour about it. For an angler there is something even better: trout lurk in some of the deeper holes. Truly the desolation of the moor is not to be found by its riversides, unless it be in their boggy cradles. Here by the young Dart is a plentiful growth of trees and luxuriance of plant life; the boulders are draped with weeds and water-mosses. There is variety also in the colouring of the lichens; and in their due season who shall describe the glory of the flaming ferns, the gold of the gorse, the purples of ling and heather? This is the moor and the river in their gentler aspects; there are times when both become a fierce passion, a wild dream, almost a horror.

It is impossible as well as undesirable to mention all the prehistoric remains that cluster so thickly on the central moorland. This is not a guidebook, and there are excellent publications, such as the writings of Mr. Crossing and the Rev. S. Baring-Gould, in which all necessary details are given.

For one of the most typical features, the clapper-bridges, we cannot claim the greatest antiquity, as the surviving specimens are on the pack-horse routes, and not on the moor's more ancient trackways. There was one at Two Bridges, but it has gone; and, still nearer to Princetown, there is one over the Ockery, a rugged structure of unwrought boulders, to which later parapets have been added. The true Dartmoor bridge has no parapet. One of the finest is at Postbridge, in the very heart of the moor; there are others at Teign Head and Dartmeet. In these bridges the huge "clappers" or blocks of granite lie absolutely unmorticed. Two of the horizontal blocks at

Postbridge are about fifteen feet in length. At Scaur Hill there is a bridge of a single massive boulder. Though essentially characteristic of Dartmoor, there are similar bridges elsewhere, as at Torr Steps over the Exmoor Barle, and in the Peak district.

Another special interest attaches to Postbridge: it is here that the ghostly and indistinct Lych Way starts on its route to Lydford church. By this track in old days burial parties carried their dead to Lydford, which is still the parish church of a larger section of the moorland. Before the year 1260 Lydford had to be resorted to for all religious purposes; from that date permission was given to inhabitants of the eastern moors to use the church of Widecombe. In days before education had done something to kill picturesque imaginings, it is not surprising that many a phantom cortege was supposed to wend its way along this haunted track; and the moor folk were very careful not to pass that way alone at night-time. But the ghosts have been laid now, or men's eyes are sealed by their incredulity; the only night-haunters of Dartmoor are mist, and rain, and storm.

In making a tour of the border villages it is natural to begin with Lydford, the mother-parish, which, with an extent of 56,333 acres, claims to be the largest parish in England. Lydford boasts of importance even as far back as the Roman invasion, but this is very dubious; there is no sign of anything Roman either at Lydford or on the moorland. The town was burnt by the Danes in 997, when they also destroyed Tavistock Abbey. It is certain that Lydford ranked high among the Stannary towns, and was a place of consequence. Its castle, dating from soon after the Conquest, is by no means imposing in its present appearance, but as a Stannary prison it had a terrible reputation. The summary justice executed by the mining and forest authorities gave rise to the term "Lydford law", which was something worse than what we now understand as lynch law. Browne, the Tavistock poet, says:

"I oft have heard of Lydford law,

How in the morn they hang and draw,

And sit in judgment after";

but it is said that even this swift treatment was better than being cast into Lydford prison.

We have to come to Lydford to find a patron saint for Dartmoor. The moor is scarce in saints, but here in the dedication of the church we find a very suitable patron in the Celtic St. Petrock, who came to Cornwall in the sixth century and founded churches at Padstow and Bodmin. There are other dedications of his on the moor borders. The present church is Perpendicular, but there are traces of a far earlier, possibly Celtic, building. The epitaph to the watchmaker Routleigh in the churchyard should be noticed. Lydford is very beautifully situated, and its ravine, down which the Lyd tumbles through steep wooded clefts, is a perpetual charm. There are two cascades, but that of Kitt's Steps is not so fine as it was once, owing to mining operations. Those who like to make comparisons may see a resemblance between Lydford Gorge and the famous Devil's Bridge of Wales, and they will probably have to admit that the Welsh scene is the grander; but Lydford is very lovely for all that, and its stream is a true child of the moorland. This ravine of the Lyd was once infested by a gang of vicious savages known as the Gubbins. There have been similar reversions to primitive barbarism even within the past century, people inhabiting mud huts and living chiefly by robbing the moormen of their cattle. It is probable that the Doones of Exmoor, though glorified by Blackmore, were simply robbers of this rude type.

Lydford also has a story of a traveller whose horse once cleared the gorge at a leap, the bridge having fallen; the rider, unconscious of his peril, was thus borne to safety across the roaring torrent of the chasm. But the summer visitor must not expect to find the Lyd a roaring torrent.

There are some fine tors near Lydford, though not the highest of the moorland. Brent Tor is singularly picturesque, and is a notable landmark by reason of the Early England church on its summit. The hill was fortified in early times, traces of stone and earthwork remaining; and there is a legend, as so often with high-standing churches, that the devil resented the church being built on what he considered his special domain, but was discomfited by the erection being placed under the patronage of St.

Michael. The rock itself is volcanic, so that the Prince of Darkness had a reason for deeming it his private property. The church is said to have been built as a thankoffering for deliverance from the sea. Those who reach it have to do so by a steep and stony path, which we may take, if we will, as a symbol; and it is often difficult to stand in the graveyard because of the fierce winds that beat upon it. In times of storm it might be easy to imagine that St. Michael and the spirits of darkness were waging their ancient conflict. Not many worshippers in England can boast that they attend a church 1130 feet above sea level; but the church at Princetown is higher still. Perhaps it is not surprising that a more accessible church has been built at North Brent Tor, yet after coming here it would seem like a lapse in manhood to attend the other.

As we get northward of Lydford we approach the region of Dartmoor's greatest heights. At Bairdown, near Hare Tor, there is a finely-placed monolith or menhir; but the view from Great Lynx Tor is more impressive than any prehistoric remains can be, and includes both the English and the Bristol Channels. Mist and rain may often obscure the outlook, but there are clear times when the waters beyond Plymouth Sound can be seen to the south, while to the north glimmers the Severn Sea where it meets the Atlantic Ocean. The two highest tors lie beyond Lynx—Yes Tor and High Willhayes; both of these, though High Willhayes has a slight advantage, are well over 2000 feet.

The grand Tavy Cleave, one of the famous beauty spots of the moor, is just south of Amicombe Hill. The Tavy, one of the many rivers that spring from the morasses around Cranmere, here tumbles—in summer a cooling stream, in winter an impetuous torrent—among scattered boulders and crags at the foot of the bare hills. Very different is this scene from Lydford Gorge, but far more typically moorland. There is no woodland here, but the gaunt flanks of granite upheavals, and a restless stream gushing through stark lichened rocks. Grim summits cap the ravine; below are bogs that in wet seasons may be formidable.

Of the peril of losing one's way on Dartmoor we learn something when we come to Amicombe Hill. Here are the stones known as Bronescombe's Loaf and Cheese, which call to memory an adventure of Bronescombe, Bishop of Exeter in the thirteenth century, whose tomb is in the Cathedral. He was much beloved of the people, and the part that he plays in folklore proves how strongly he impressed his personality upon them. It is said that the bishop and his chaplain lost their way in crossing the moorland, and at last found themselves on Amicombe Hill. Tired and hungry, the former said to his companion: "Our Master, when tempted in the wilderness, was offered bread created from the stones. If the same offer was made to me, I doubt if I could refuse."

"Bread with a hunch of cheese as well," suggested the equally hungry chaplain.

"Ah," sighed the bishop, "I could not hold out against bread and cheese!"

While he was still speaking, a limping moorman suddenly appeared, with a wallet on his back, and the chaplain eagerly asked if he had any food to give them.

"Aye," replied the man, "I have some bread and cheese—naught else."

"Give it to us, my son," exclaimed the bishop. "I will repay thee well." But the stranger answered that he desired no payment; he only asked that the bishop would alight from his pony and doff his cap, saluting him as master. The bishop was about to comply, when his comrade noticed that one of the stranger's feet had a curious appearance. In great alarm he cried to the bishop, who hurriedly made the sign of the cross. Immediately the stranger vanished, and the loaf and cheese that he had produced were converted into the stones that we see here.

It is a fashion to go to Cranmere, and even to leave a card as proof that the visit has been paid; but the bogs and mires that surround it always make the approach difficult—in wet seasons dangerous; and except as the source of so many Devon rivers the spot is really unattractive. It is never more than a marshy pool, and sometimes scarcely that. Dartmoor is one of the rainiest spots in England, its height being swept by the moisture-laden winds from both seas; and the rainfall is held in its high-lying hollows by peat bogs. Every hollow is like a granite cup, and where there is not the immediate granite, there is the equally impervious china-clay of its denudations; these basins are perpetually fed by rain or mists, and the rivers thus born never run dry. From the actual pool of Cranmere rises the West Ockment, while the East Ockment, the Tavy, the Dart, the Taw, and the Teign spring from morasses or quags in its neighbourhood. No other spot in the kingdom gives birth to so many rivers of importance—important for their great beauty though only slightly for their navigation. On the moor itself they are rapid streams, sometimes peat-stained, yet always limpid; and this rapidity, especially after rainfall, goes with them to their estuaries, bringing sometimes sudden and dangerous risings of tide. The general Dartmoor watershed is southward; all the streams but the Ockments and the Taw flow to the English Channel. Teignmouth, Dartmouth, Plymouth, are watered by Dartmoor rivers.

Though the mother and nurse of these rivers, Cranmere is disappointing; yet it has loomed large in local folklore. Like Dosmare of the Bodmin Moors, it has been supposed to be bottomless; and the fate of doomed spirits has been to drain it with a leaky shell. One tale is of an old farmer who, after death, here had to expiate his misdoings. His ghost was so troublesome that it took seven parsons to secure it. Being changed into a colt by their pious spells, a servant lad was told to lead him to Cranmere pool, take off the halter, and leave the place instantly, without glancing back. The boy obeyed all the instructions but the last; and on looking back he received a parting kick from the colt, which then plunged into the pool in the form of a ball of fire.

We are indebted to the Ockment Rivers for the name of Okehampton (in Domesday the name is Ochementone), which is perhaps the best centre from which to explore the northern moorland. But the peacefulness and to some extent the security of the district have been affected by the fact that ninety acres of land are leased for the use of the Royal Horse and Field Artillery, whose practice has sometimes jeopardized unwary tourists. Happily the character of Dartmoor saves it from becoming a huge camp and review-ground, like Salisbury Plain; but it needs some patriotism to forgive such military occupation as we find at Okehampton and elsewhere.

The ruins of the castle, on the site of a Celtic settlement, are well placed above the river, surrounded by trees whose foliage is a delight after the barren uplands. Every lover of beauty appreciates the difference between a wooded district and a treeless waste; and this is usually the emphatic distinction between the central moor and its borders. It was a real privilege that allowed some of the French prisoners to reside at Okehampton instead of at Princetown, and a few of their tombs will be found in the churchyard here, so long after it has ceased to matter.

There is older tradition here also. Those who are abroad at night-time will do well to avoid meeting the ghostly equipage of Lady Howard, which drives nightly between the castle and Fitzford. Lady Howard was a much-married woman, daughter of the unhappy Fitz of Fitzford, and her last husband was the infamous Richard Grenville, who sullied a name otherwise greatly ennobled. She chose to retain the title of her third husband, and under this designation popular fancy has dealt very unkindly with her. Her doom is to drive each night to Okehampton Castle in her coach made of dead men's bones—the bones of her murdered husbands, as slander tells; and her phantom hound plucks a single blade of grass from the castle mound. When all the grass has been plucked, her doom will cease. An old Devonshire ballad tells us of her:

"My ladye's coach hath nodding plumes,

The driver hath no head;

My ladye is an ashen white,

As one that long is dead".

It is considered ill-omened to meet this lady, and those who would avoid doing so, as well as evade the firing, may find a pleasant refuge at Belstone, at Sticklepath, or at South Zeal. Belstone has a tor of 1568 feet in height, and also some standing-stones named the Nine Maidens, with their fallen piper. The girls were thus doomed and changed into stone as a punishment for dancing on Sunday. Though their piper is displaced and mutilated, they still dance each day at noon—for those whose faith is equal to the demand. Belstone is one of several "Bels" in the Dartmoor country, such as

Bellever and Bel Tor, but we have yet to learn that they have any connection with Baal, in spite of all the nonsense that has been talked.

At Sticklepath, a charmingly pretty village with beautiful flower-gardens, there is a holy well with a curiously inscribed stone; while at South Zeal, near a quaint belfry, is an interesting wayside cross. There are some delightful old houses in the neighbourhood, usually manorial in their origin and now turned into farms, such as North Wyke, West Wyke, and Wykington. It is from this side that the ascent of Cosdon Beacon is often made—Cosdon, sometimes called Cawsand, being noted for the fine stone-rows and other immemorial relics to be found on its slopes. The Beacon has been introduced to literature by novels of Mr. Baring-Gould and Mr. Phillpotts. We are reminded also of fiction—the familiar pages of Westward Ho!—by the name of the Oxenham Arms, preserving the memory of a famous old Devon family, the Oxenhams, with their tradition of the white bird.

By whatever way we pass from Okehampton or South Tawton to Chagford, we are delayed on all sides by numberless spots of beauty or interest. The main road, which branches to Exeter, is served by a motor bus from Moreton, but familiarity with the moorland can never be gained by proceeding along a highroad, whether on foot or awheel. Many as are the remaining standing-stones, circles, and pounds, those that have been destroyed were far more numerous; but the finest monument of the "old people" is rarely as attractive as the natural beauties that surround many of them, and only the professed antiquarian will care to examine them all with patient study. To most of us they are only bare stones. They are so ancient that the human interest has died from them. But we find this human touch at such places as Wonson manor house, now a farm, where an ace of diamonds painted on the woodwork of a bedroom reminds us of a former squire, who had it placed there in order that he might curse it each night for the ruin it had brought him in his gambling.

Gidleigh, which is near, stands high, and has a fine park of oak, birch, and mountain-ash, with ferns and whortles in a rock-strewn undergrowth. Its colouring is especially rich in the fall of the year, with the lovely fading of ferns, the purple of heath, and the red of berries. The North Teign dashes foamingly below, fretful and rock-thwarted. This is really a more beautiful spot than ever was the Holy Street Mill that Creswick and other artists painted; plenty of picturesque mills may be found throughout the country, but scenes of such loveliness are rare. The rhododendrons in bloom add much to the beauty of Gidleigh, which also boasts a small castle with whose ruinous walls the ash trees have incorporated themselves.

At Teign Head (not quite the head of the river) is one of the moorland's clapper bridges; but Leigh Bridge, where the two Teigns meet, though of the common single-arch type, is more charming because its surroundings are wooded. The two rivers unite before reaching Chagford, and beyond that modernized and popular little resort the Teign passes out of the confines of the moor altogether. But at Fingle Bridge, one of the most famous Devon beauty-spots, something of moorland wildness still remains. Almost the whole course of the Teign is of remarkable beauty. It here passes the fine trees of Whiddon Park till it comes to a ravine every yard of which seems to be prehistoric dust. There are earthworks and camps on both sides; while not far off is the great dolmen or cromlech of Drewsteignton, near the small Bradmere pool.

Ancient camps are not common on the actual moorland, but we find them here at the fringe: those Bronze Age moormen appear to have been peaceable among themselves, and only to have raised entrenchments against external enemies. Possibly this lovely valley of the Teign saw a desperate struggle between tribes of an early and a newer civilization, one of the primitive race-strifes that shaped our people. Now it is a haunt of the country-lover and the tourist, many of whom deplore that the banks and hollows have been denuded of their rarer ferns by the depredations of thoughtless visitors. But nothing has killed the charm of the tumbling torrent, the stained massy boulders, the pools and shallows. It is little wonder that Chagford has become a popular holiday place; yet its miry condition in winter was best expressed by the pithy comment of its sarcastic neighbours—"Chaggy-vord—Good Lord!" The "Three Crowns", of which Kingsley spoke as a "beautiful old mullioned and gabled Perpendicular inn", was once a manor house.

From Chagford we reach the open moorland by climbing Tincombe (Teigncombe) Hill, and we must follow the South Teign if we wish to examine the Fernworthy circle or the Grey Wethers. But we shall probably be more attracted by what was once a genuine moor town, as its name implies. Moreton Hampstead, no longer properly on the moor, though it once was, is the starting-place of the single true road that leads across Dartmoor, passing Two Bridges on its way to Buckland, Tavistock, and Plymouth. The ancient central trackway, which is far older, being connected with the Fosseway, also ran from Moreton. Though linked to great roads from the shires, there is nothing to show that the Romans ever used this track, or that they ever entered Dartmoor at all.

Perhaps Moreton is an even better centre for visiting the moor than Chagford, and it is quite as attractive in itself, with its interesting but despoiled church, and its fine arcaded almshouses, dating from 1637. The inhabitants, however, deplore the loss of their old "dancing-tree", an elm growing from the mutilated base of a granite cross. This tree was supposed to be over 300 years old, and it succumbed a few years since to age and many infirmities. Balls and concerts were given on a platform built on the massive branches. The tree has received literary honour in Blackmore'sChristowell. It is from Moreton that we can best reach Grimspound, with its twenty-four hut-circles. The pound encloses about four acres, surrounded by a double wall of granite blocks. Scattered in the neighbourhood are other hut-circles, barrows, and stone alignments.

Bowerman's Nose (Celtic veor-maen, or great stone) is nearer to Manaton; it is a natural freak of weathered granite, 40 feet in height, standing at an elevation of about 1300 feet above sea level. Many foolish conjectures have been magnified into supposed fact by those who have taken this and other Dartmoor features to be the work of man. Manaton itself, with its own tor rising behind the church, is a beautiful little village, rendered more lovely by the River Bovey.

It is the fall of the Becka brook into the Bovey that provides the popular Becky Falls; but in summer, as Mr. Baring-Gould says, this is rather a water trickle than a waterfall; in autumn and winter, when fewer visitors see it, the stream is a turbulent torrent. Not far distant is the beautiful Lustleigh Cleave, which though not on the moor is thoroughly moorland in its character and its antiquities. So hugely piled are the boulders at its foot that the river is generally quite out of sight, to be heard but not seen.

But to get to a typical moorland parish we must not linger at Lustleigh; we must go out to Widecombe, and by whatever road we reach it we shall understand the sad fate of Tom Pearce's old mare. Widecombe is in a hollow surrounded by heights and tors (it must be understood that the word tor is only used where the granite actually protrudes from the soil). Bel, Rippon, and Hey Tors are on one side, Hamildon Down on the other. The valley, which is only low in comparison with the surrounding hills, was much worked in days out of date by the tin-streamers, and there is a plentiful growth of pines and sycamores above the traces they left.

The village is a small thing, but it looms large in moorland traditions, not only because of its famous sheep fair, nor because its church is the finest on Dartmoor, but because the Devil himself paid the spot some very personal attentions at one time, and indeed was once reported to have lived here. It was on an October Sunday in the year 1638 that a stranger riding through Poundsgate enquired the way to Widecombe, and, being given a drink, it was noticed that the liquor actually hissed as it passed down his throat. The folk were gathered at afternoon service when there came on a great darkness, followed, as Prince tells us, by a "terrible and fearful thunder, like the noise of many guns, accompanied with dreadful lightning, to the great amazement of the people, the darkness still increasing that they could not see each other". Ere long there came an extraordinary flame, filling the church with a "loathsome smell like brimstone", and a ball of fire fell through the roof. The folk all dropped terror-stricken to the floor. A large beam hurled itself down between the parson and the clerk, yet neither was hurt; others were less fortunate, four being killed and sixty-two injured. At last a man ventured to propose: "Shall we go out from the church?" but the parson answered: "Let us make an end of prayer, for it is better to die here than in another place".

There is little in the present building to recall this terrible visitation, in which it is clear that a most violent thunderstorm has assumed a permanent place in Devonshire folklore; but its story is told in a versified narrative hanging on the tower wall. This tower, though certainly struck by lightning on the occasion, was not destroyed; and it remains, reaching the height of 120 feet, a model of impressive Perpendicular. The woodwork of the roof is also excellent, and the surviving pictured panels show how fine the screen was before being cut down in 1827. So large a church seems to indicate a thicker population in early days, perhaps when the tin working was at its best; and it is stated that the tower itself was erected voluntarily by successful tinners.

At the September fair there is still a lively gathering of moor sheep, moor horses, and moormen, and the chatter has a rich Devonian intonation, with a delightful smack of the soil. Widecombe is one of the so-called Venville parishes, Venville being a word of doubtful origin (sometimes written Wangfield), which probably signifies a kind of feudal tenure. These parishes were freehold with certain attached services, and their inhabitants had a prescriptive right to all uses of the moorland except those of "vert and venison"—that is, of gathering green wood or killing the deer. There was never much green wood to gather on the moor itself, and the deer have long since departed, unless when one occasionally wanders over from Exmoor. The moorland proper, technically the Forest, is surrounded by commons, outside which are the Venville parishes; and these commons were formerly of far wider extent, having been sadly curtailed by "newtakes" and enclosures, sometimes by the authorities of the Duchy, sometimes by lords of the different manors, sometimes by moor-settlers themselves. A small fee is demanded by the Duchy for all cattle pastured on the moor by outsiders, the cattle of the moormen grazing free; and there are periodical "drifts", when each Venville proprietor claims his own, and "foreigners" have to pay the tax.

We are reminded of London by the dedication of Widecombe Church, which is to St. Pancras; and thoughts of the metropolis again come to us at Hey Tor, which provided granite for London and Waterloo Bridges. These eastern heights, Rippon and Hey Tors, are not so lofty as those of the north-west, but they both command very fine views. It is magnificent to see sunset flame across the moors from this eastern borderland. Patches of cultivation, open moorland dotted with sheep, lovely river-valleys, and wide undulations of heather and gorse fade into horizons of the westward summits. There is always the changeful charm of atmosphere. The scene may be of vast, glorious peacefulness, but it is great also when there is the confusion of cloud-strife, rain raking the hillsides—when the spirit of the moor is abroad in storm and darkness, when colour is quenched in wet and driving wrack. It is easy then to picture the moor as the phantasmal haunt of lost races. Dartmoor has many moods, variable as the soul of man—sometimes of gentle pensiveness and dreaming, touched with sentiment, sometimes of fierce striving passion or inconsolable woe, sometimes of desolation deepened to despair. In all these there is a quality of the unconventional and untamed, a sense of the nearness of mystery, the brooding of the unseen, the force of powers that we sometimes feel to be in profoundest sympathy with our own longings and imaginings, sometimes in the most vexed antagonism. Here, as elsewhere, we find very much what we bring, but we find it intensified, vivified; it may lure us as a kindly home, or repel us as a desert. Even the repulsion has its own manner of charm, because it braces us to self-assertion and manhood.

It was from this Hey Tor side of the moorland that William Howitt once looked forth upon Dartmoor. He tells us: "My road wound up and up, the heather and the bilberry on either hand shewing me that cultivation had never disturbed the soil they grew in; and one sole woodlark from the far-ascending forest to the right filled the wild solitude with his autumnal note. At that moment I reached an eminence, and at once saw the dark crags of Dartmoor high aloft before me, and one large solitary house in the valley beneath the woods. So fair, so silent, save for the woodlark's note and the moaning river, so unearthly did the whole scene seem, that my imagination delighted to look upon it as an enchanted land, and to persuade itself that that house stood as it would stand for ages, under the spell of silence but beyond the reach of death and change." This was written three-quarters of a century since, before nature had begun greatly to inspire our prose writers; and for its period it is very creditable. In poetry we have made no progress; but in the prose literature of nature—that is to say, of natural scenes viewed under human emotion—it is an immense step from the writings of William Gilpin and Richard Warner, and even of Howitt, to those of George Borrow and Richard Jefferies. Even in prose it had been the poets, Gray and Wordsworth, who had shown the way, very slowly followed. Warner was an enterprising and intelligent traveller, and visited many parts of the south and west from his Bath home, long before the time of railways. It is interesting to notice how he was daunted by Dartmoor. Overnight he had decided to walk from Lydford to Two Bridges, though the idea of "travelling twelve miles over a desolate moor, wild as the African Syrtes, without a single human inhabitant or regular track, had something in it very deterring". Next morning it actually deterred. "As the trial approximated, my resolution, like Acres' courage, gradually oozed away, and before breakfast was finished I had dropped the idea, and determined to take a circuitous route by Oakhampton." His landlord had just told him how the body of a dead sailor had been discovered in a lonely spot, where it must have lain for weeks; and Warner's discretion proved greater than his valour.

But we need not sneer at him. It is still easy to be lost on Dartmoor.

Those who are fond of logan-stones may find some in this district: there is one at Lustleigh, a fine one on Rippon, and others elsewhere. Some of them no longer "log" satisfactorily, and certainly none are connected with Druidic or other ceremonial. They are natural formations, like the rock-basins and the tors themselves.

It is more interesting to pass on to one of the loveliest portions of the moorland border, that which is watered by the Rivers Dart after their junction at Dartmeet. We have already seen the West Dart at Two Bridges, and the East Dart should be explored at least to Postbridge. It is especially beautiful where it is joined by the Walla, at the foot of Yes Tor. Dartmeet is a small settlement of houses, and deserves to be popular, for while quite on the moorland it has none of the desolate aspect that some persons find depressing, and those who love woods can get them to perfection around Holne and Buckland. Tourists who have been up the river from Dartmouth to Totnes are inclined to think that they know the Dart; they are as much mistaken as those who think they know the Wye when they have been to Symond's Yat. To know the Dart its moorland recesses must be explored, where the stream is in its fresh impetuous youth; below Totnes, though its banks are undoubtedly lovely, it has become chastened and sobered. At the junction of the Wallabrook with the Dart is a very fine view of Yar Tor, near which is the luxuriant Brimpts plantation.

The meeting of the two Darts is in a low rock-strewn gorge, to appreciate which the roadway must be left. Near is the Coffin-stone, with its inscribed crosses, used as a resting-place for the dead on their way to burial. It is said that when a man of notorious wickedness was being carried to his grave, his coffin as usual was rested on this stone, and a flash of fire struck downward from a passing cloud, consuming the body and splitting the solid rock. The cleft remains as a proof. The rocks of this district are frequently of metallic substance, and are often struck by lightning; perhaps this kills the romance of the legend.

Buckland-in-the-Moor, so called to distinguish it from other Bucklands, is not strictly on the moorland at all, and is cradled in woodland; it is a very small, delightful village, close to the united Webburns, which join the Dart below. The river here flows in most tortuous fashion under the beautiful woods of Buckland Drive and Holne Chase. Holne Cot has a place in literature as the birthplace of Charles Kingsley, in 1819, but he left it when an infant. Another literary remembrance is the birth of the dramatist Ford at Ilsington, and Tavistock had a true poet in William Browne; but it must be confessed that the literary glories of the moorland are not great, and Carrington, its special poet, is quite a third-rate writer. There has been no Wordsworth to interpret Dartmoor. We have to come to modern fiction, in the books of Mr. Baring-Gould and Mr. Phillpotts, for anything like an adequate literary treatment; and even in this department there has been no Lorna Doone.

At Holne and Buckland may be found some of the most luxuriant woodland of the moor-borders, yellow with dense primroses in the spring. On both sides of the river there are rich woods of birch and oak and fir, while in the valley through which the Dart runs are fertile succulent marshes, beautified with bogbeans, asphodels, and sundews, and with the exquisite Osmunda regalis flourishing where, happily, it is very difficult to reach. In parts the river flows through ivied crags, above which hang clusters of mountain-ash. There are prehistoric remains at Holne and at Hembury, but it is difficult to think of the past where the present is of such insistent charm. Moor, woodland, river, stone-strewn waste and fertile pasture here meet, with no discord or violent contrast, but harmonized by a reconciling atmosphere of beauty. The churches both at Buckland and Holne have very interesting screens, and at Holne is a finely-carved wooden pulpit.

Though it can scarcely be said to belong to the moors, Ashburton is a good starting-point for the examination of the eastern moorlands. Here and at Buckfastleigh are the only remains of the once extensive Devon woollen manufactures; and Ashburton was also at one time a Stannary town. It has a good church and many interesting associations, but we cannot linger either here or at Buckfast, where a settlement of Benedictines has restored the old abbey.

There is a great temptation to stay awhile at Dean Prior for the sake of Robert Herrick, one of England's sweetest lyrists, who was twice vicar here, being presented by Charles I in 1629, dispossessed at the Commonwealth, and reinstated at the Restoration. He abused the neighbourhood so heartily in his verse that it is surprising he should have accepted the living a second time; but perhaps he said a little more than he meant. The exact spot of his burial in the churchyard is unknown. Some of Herrick's lyrics are so lovely that even Devonians must forgive him, though he wrote:

"O men, O manners; now and ever known

To be a rocky generation,

A people currish, churlish as the seas,

And rude almost as rudest savages;

With whom I did and may re-sojourn when

Rocks turn to rivers, rivers turn to men".

As he returned voluntarily to this exile, we must imagine the miracle to have taken place, or perhaps his own heart had been tamed by his adversity.

The southern moor is watered by beautiful but less familiar rivers than those of the west and east; the Avon, the Erme, the Yealm have all their own charm, and are as genuinely children of Dartmoor as the Teign, the Dart, or the Tavy. Probably the best centre for this district is South Brent, where there is a church that has been badly treated by restoration. Brent Hill, rising to about 1000 feet, must not be confused with Brent Tor. Both are strikingly conspicuous hills, but this southern height no longer boasts its chapel dedicated to St. Michael. The hill is a fine landmark for a large extent of country. The Avon, sometimes called the Aune, is a beautiful river, but its source in the treacherous mire of Aune Head is very dismal.

It may be worth while to tell a story told of Aune Mire by Mr. Baring-Gould, for the authenticity of which we must hold him responsible. A man was making his way through the bog "when he came on a top-hat reposing, brim downwards, on the sedge. He gave it a kick, whereupon a voice called out from beneath, 'What be you a-doin' to my 'at?' The man replied, 'Be there now a chap under'n?' 'Ees, I reckon,' was the reply, 'and a hoss under me likewise.'" This is a fair representation of the swallowing capacity of Dartmoor mires, and they should certainly be avoided by any strangers without an expert guide.

The Avon on its southward course passes the old Abbots' Way, the track of the monks from Buckfast to Tavistock. A good deal of the path can still be traced. Approaching Shipley Bridge, the river becomes very lovely, shadowed by Shipley and Black Tors, and flowing beneath a bridge of single span among rocks, trees, and ferns. Not many tourists come hither, and the result is greater wealth of specimens—mountain and lady ferns, false maidenhair, various hart's tongues.

The beautiful situation of Didworthy might make one in love with farming; and there are numberless remains here for those who wish to be in touch with the "old people". This is one aspect that is always present, from end to end of Dartmoor—the silent tokens of vanished peoples; they may be absolutely intrusive if we choose, or they may blend, scarcely noticed, with the natural features of their surroundings. Some persons will come and think of nothing else; but to those who come with wider purpose the old stones and memorials give a hint of far-off human interest, softening the harshness of the wilder scenes, and enriching the gentler with a touch of pathos. The solitude of places where man has been is always different from that of untrodden wildernesses.

The Avon runs beneath another lovely bridge when it comes to South Brent, which is locally noted for its fairs and pannier market, and is a favourite resort with excursionists from Plymouth. The curious winding streets of the little town are in perfect accord with their setting. At Wrangaton, not far distant, are the links of the South Devon Golf Club; but this is only one of the many opportunities that golfers have of exercising their sport on Dartmoor or in its immediate neighbourhood. It is fairly evident that a considerable section of the public to-day will go nowhere unless accompanied by its golf clubs, and certainly the game often introduces these people to much beautiful scenery that they might otherwise miss. They must decide themselves as to which is the real attraction.

There are several other river sources not far from that of Avon—Erme Head, Yealm Head, Plym Head; this cluster of bogs almost rivals the cradle of rivers at Cranmere. The Erme valley and plains are thickly strewn with prehistoric relics and traces of old tin workings; but, well populated as this district must once have been, it is now one of the most lonely and desolate parts of the moorland. Dreary as the Erme may be at its source, however, it develops to great beauty during its brief course to the sea, issuing at Mothecombe, in a series of windings and wooded reaches, with a swiftness of tide that tells its moorland birth. The general public makes the river's acquaintance at Ivybridge; otherwise it is by no means a familiar stream.

At Harford, which is practically a moorland parish, we have a church dedicated to St. Petrock, like those of South Brent and Lydford, emphasizing his claim to be the patron of Dartmoor. The chief heights in this region are the Three Barrows, Staldon, and Sharp Tor. Perhaps the most remarkable of the moor's stone avenues starts from a circle on Stall Moor, and terminates with a kistvaen not far from Aune Head. There are other stone rows near, all of which have been partially despoiled, but less so than elsewhere; the mystery of their significance remains unsolved. Ugborough Beacon and Butterton Hill, both about 1200 feet in height, stand like southern sentinels of the moorland to the east of Harford. On the slopes of Sharp Tor is a stunted wood, very like Wistman's.

Westward, near Cornwood, is the ravine of the River Yealm, known as Awns and Dendles, which it is best not to visit on Plymouth's early-closing day or on Bank Holidays. It is a pity that popularity should mean vulgarizing, for it is right that every lovely spot should be accessible to the greatest possible number of those who can appreciate it. The qualification is an important one; nothing is gained by the thronging to such scenes of those whose tastes are best met by entertainment pavilions and roundabouts. Besides which, the conscienceless tripper is a terror to all who love ferns, and there are still some rarities to be found in the Yealm valley.

Near Cornwood is Fardell, once a manor of the Raleighs; and though Sir Walter was not born here he undoubtedly paid the spot many visits. The place is also interesting because of a stone discovered here, bearing Ogham inscriptions supposed to prove the extent of the Irish invasion somewhere about the sixth century, when Devon and Cornwall were overrun by saints and chieftains from the green island. There are a number of attractive manor houses in this part of the moorland's fringe, together with some fine heights, such as Pen Beacon and Shell Tor, rising to about 1500 feet. But there is no particular charm in the china-clay works of Lee Moor—an industry which may be studied on a larger scale in the St. Austell district of

Cornwall. China-clay, or kaolin, is a detritus of granite, much used for pottery and in the preparation of calicoes; partly also for the supposed white sugar of confectionery and in cheap adulterated flours. The neighbourhoods of its workings are as white as those of coal are black, and in this respect china-clay must be given the preference; but neither tends to beautify a district.

None of the lovely rivers already mentioned water a town of any great importance; but when we come to the Plym it is different. The Plym is not the most beautiful of Dartmoor streams, but it has given its name to Plymouth, and Plymouth has imposed its own title on the three towns which united form the supreme naval and industrial centre of the west country. Other western seaports have decayed rather than advanced—they have deteriorated at least in their relative importance; but Plymouth has advanced and is still advancing. In no sense does it belong to Dartmoor, but the Plym and the Tavy, whose waters go to swell Plymouth Sound, are both genuine children of the moorland. The Plym, rising not far from the Yealm, makes its way to its junction with the Meavy through a grand ravine, overshadowed by the Dewerstone. Before reaching the Dewerstone, however, the river passes under the Cadover (or Cadaford) Bridge, and from this circumstance there has been some dispute as to whether the true name of the stream should not be the Cad. Carrington gave it this name, but he cannot be taken as an authority; and it is probable that the cad in Cadover is simply a corruption of the Celtic word coed, or wood, and has nothing to do with the river at all. From Cadover to Shaugh Bridge are some wonderfully beautiful scenes, banks strewn with granite fragments amidst tangled undergrowth. The Dewerstone towering above is appropriately the haunt of a demon huntsman of the moors, who careers abroad on stormy nights with his fierce-eyed baying wish-hounds.

Whether we pursue the Meavy upward from the bridge or follow the united rivers through the exquisite Bickleigh vale, there is much loveliness; but there are times when Bickleigh valley is too popular to be pleasant, unless our chief study is human nature. We can best study human nature in the towns; and we do not want to be pursued by its noisier manifestations amid scenes that call for the sympathetic presence of peace. Shaugh Prior, finely placed on the border of the moorland, is entirely delightful, as also is Meavy, with its famous oak, twenty-five feet in girth, and its village cross. Lovers of such things will specially notice the old font-cover of the church at Shaugh. There is also a notable cross on the slope of Ringmore Down, over eight feet in height, the tallest on the moor.

One of the pleasantest spots of this corner of Dartmoor is the village of Sheepstor, a familiar sight from the railway to all who are making the journey to Princetown by train. It lies at a little distance from the rail, but the Burrator reservoir here constructed for the supply of Plymouth, in the bed of an ancient lake, probably draws more curious visitors than do the beauty and interest of its surroundings. Sheepstor Church has been unhappily restored, to the sad detriment of its exquisite screen, enough of which has been preserved to tell of its original glory. The tor itself rises finely above the clustering cottages of the village, and a cavern called the Pixies' Cave is shown as the refuge of one of the Elford family during the Civil War. It is said that he lay concealed here, somewhat in the manner of the Baron Bradwardine's concealment in Scott's Waverley, while the Roundhead troopers were closely searching his house and grounds, at Langstone by Burrator. Having won the affection of the peasantry, they kept his secret and provided him with food. It is said that he occupied his enforced leisure by painting the sides of the cave, but no traces of painting can now be seen. The cave is difficult to find, and nothing but treachery could have revealed the hiding-place. It is not stated whether Elford's presence drove out the pixies to whom the cavern really belonged; but in case they still remain it is well to remember the usual etiquette of leaving a pin or some other small gift. Pixies seem to be as easily pleased as are the patron saints of some holy wells.

A remarkable story is told by Mrs. Bray as to the manner in which the cholera reached Sheepstor during the terrible visitation of 1832. A man of supposed poverty died, with his wife and children, at Plymouth, where the plague was raging fiercely, and their home was visited by two brothers, with small hope of picking up anything valuable. To their surprise a large sum in cash was found, and the brothers fought together over the dead bodies in order to possess it. While fighting, they were disturbed by the police, and one of the two, having actually assumed some of the clothes of the dead man, took refuge in a cottage at Sheepstor. Strangely enough, he escaped the infection himself, but it was taken by the two worthy cottagers, and they both died. Their little boy, thus orphaned, carried word to Tavistock that his parents had both died and that he had been left alone with the dead. It was considered so remarkable that the cholera should have visited so healthy a spot, and especially people of such known cleanliness, that an enquiry was instituted and the story came out.

Before leaving Sheepstor something should be said of the fine stone rows and other remains at Drizzlecombe, but it is impossible here to give full attention to these numerous relics. We find a reminder of the Elford family in the name of Yelverton, a corruption of Elford-town. Yelverton and Dousland have both become popular with residents and visitors, having the convenience of rail and commanding a district of great beauty. But, attractive as they are, neither can claim to be on the moorland, nor can this claim be made by Tavistock itself, though that town boasts of being the "western gate of Dartmoor". There is a rich supply of beauty and of delightful associations at Tavistock, but it was never a moor town. Here and at Buckland Monachorum are many traces of the two rival abbeys, of which Tavistock was far the more ancient and the more wealthy. Both spots have memories of Francis Drake, and at Tavistock there is an admirable statue. Buckland and Buckfast, being both Cistercian, had much communication; and the influence of these three abbeys was great in preserving the moorland trackways, setting up crosses for the guidance of travellers, and keeping the moor open to a gradual course of civilization. They were also centres of art and culture at a period when such things were at a discount, and in this respect we can never be too grateful to the old monastic settlements. Whether or not we class them among those good things whose corruption is worst, they were undoubtedly good in their day. We find around Dartmoor as elsewhere that the monks chose their localities well, with a keen eye for natural beauty and the advantages of water. We may infer also that they ventured across Dartmoor when other men were chary of crossing it, and their faith had certainly the courage of its convictions. If we meet their ghosts along the Abbots' Way by night we need not fear that they will be other than kindly. If they are ghosts now, there was a time when they drove forth ghosts themselves, and when they converted pagan monuments into symbols of the religion of love.

It would be very pleasant to linger about Tavistock, with its bright river that we met in our rambles from Lydford; but the moorland calls us. There is another lovely river, the Walla or Walkham (Walkham is probably Walla-combe), which lures us to one of the most fascinating regions of Dartmoor. The poet Browne, after the fashion of his time, wrote a narrative of the "loves of the Walla and the Tavy" in his Britannia's Pastorals; but in spite of much freshness of natural description his verses are tedious if taken in large doses, and we can leave this would-be classic legend out of the question. The stream has a typically moorland character as it flows from its source at Lynch Tor, to wind around the foot of the noble Great Mis Tor and pass beneath Merrivale Bridge. The tors of this district are approaching their greatest height, and Mis Tor, a true mother of storms, is one of the most magnificent. Merrivale bridge is on the highroad from Tavistock to Princetown, little frequented since the opening of the railway, and surely there are few finer bits of road in the kingdom than that which here crosses the valley of the Walla, at the base of this grand tor. Whether lying in open sunshine or raked with fog and cloud, Mis Tor is always impressive, apart altogether from the rock-basins, pounds, and hut-circles that surround it. Northward of the bridge is Staple Tor; southward, nearer to the small village of Sampford Spiney, are the Vixen and Pu tors. The Vixen is a curious mass of weathered granite, taking almost any shape that the view-point and the imagination of the spectator may suggest. At Sampford there is a good Perpendicular church, and a picturesque granite-mullioned farmhouse that was once a manor. There is another good church at Walkhampton, and a fourteenth-century church-house, now the inn.

Those who are attracted to Whitchurch Down by reason of its golf links, belonging to the Tavistock Club, will see one of the most impressive old crosses of the moorland; and their sport may be combined not only with the bracing air of a high altitude but with fine views of Dartmoor and of east Cornwall. The beauty of the Walkham River is continued to its junction with the Tavy near the disused copper mine of the Virtuous Lady. Whitchurch proves its antiquity by being the Wicerce of Domesday. Its church, thus clearly dating from before the Conquest, has the lovely screen rescued by the Earl of Devon from the ill-advised restoration at Moreton Hampstead. North of Peter Tavy, a charming village in the beautiful Tavy vale, is Whit Tor, with perhaps the best walled encampment of the moorland. There are other old-world relics, such as the Langstone menhir. And so we arrive once more at Lydford.

Surely there can be few spots of such comparatively small size that so teem with interest and fascination as Dartmoor. In the number of its prehistoric remains it is only equalled by parts of Cornwall, and their preservation is owing to thinness of modern population. We may imagine that most of England was once scattered with similar traces of dead peoples, but in most places these have been eradicated by successive waves of population. Dartmoor has been left in solitude, and though its few inhabitants have done their best to remove or mutilate the immemorial monuments, enough have been overlooked to furnish us with a wide treasure ground. But where the antiquarian will come to measure and dig and conjecture, the artist, the poet, the lover of nature will find many other things to allure. The sportsman will also come here, especially the angler, who finds excellent trout, though the fish are not often large. Perhaps happily, only the few main roads are available for motor traffic, but during the summer these are much frequented; there are also many excursion cars and chars-à-bancs to the more popular beauty-spots, starting from places like Moreton, Chagford, Bovey Tracey, or coming from towns far beyond the moor borders. The cyclist who does not mind dismounting at times has a wider area, and cycling on Dartmoor is not so bad as its reputation. There are some really fine stretches of road; what the rider needs is discrimination and good brakes. But he who truly wins the freedom of the moors is the pedestrian—a species not quite extinct, though discredited and often discomforted. He should come here on what we may call the divine adventure, the quest of beauty; and even on lonely Dartmoor he will find the human touch not absent.

Whoever comes, if his eyes be open, will see tracts of primitive mother earth, untamed and unsophisticated. He will see what Devon was before it was cultivated; he will be in a haunt of strange traditions, lingering superstitions, wild fancies. Perhaps when cold clammy fogs blot out the undulations and tors, a chill will strike to the heart; Dartmoor is no kindly nurse to those who have lost their way or those who are overtaken by snowfall. He who comes here must lean on his own resources; he will not be pampered and guided; he must fend for himself. Nature, as Jefferies was fond of saying, does not care for man; he is an alien, exiled by the very civilization of which he is so proud; he can do less for himself than the birds and beasts. Yet the illusion that nature does care is at times very strong; we cannot thrust it wholly from our hearts, and if we regard the earth as but the outward symbol, a mood, a thought, of some inscrutable power, we are not wrong in deeming that she responds to our deepest impulses and cravings. It is glorious poetry and it need not be bad philosophy to dream of a Being "whose dwelling is the light of setting suns"; and he who has seen a sunset flaming across Dartmoor has seen the heavens opened. He can learn also the insignificance of any single individual or race, and yet the undying importance of each if all are a part of the Godhead. Peoples have lived and died here long centuries since, leaving no memorial but grey stones; but the heather and ling are still wonderful, the gorse runs in patches of gold, the rivers sing perpetually among their lichen-stained boulders, and the soul of beauty that is ever mysterious is undying.

Such is Dartmoor, one of the few remaining tracts of uncultivated England; a region not easy to tame, offering small reward to the farmer, but rich repayment to the lovers of beauty, wildness, antiquity. There is nothing quite like it elsewhere, unless it be the Bodmin Moors of Cornwall, where the same granite asserts itself again. There is loveliness of a different sort on the moors of Yorkshire and around the Peak—on the Wiltshire, Dorset, and Sussex Downs, on the high lands or in the New Forest of Hampshire, and at spots like Hindhead in Surrey. There is still a different beauty in the fen country and the land of the Broads. But Dartmoor has its own character, which it does not surrender to a casual acquaintance; it has a reserve and depth of individuality, to be won only by slow confidence. There are strong characteristics also among the moor folk; but here a change has been in progress. It is useless to come now expecting to find a superstitious and credulous peasantry. When a district is haunted by tourist and artist, when cars and brakes unload crowds of chattering sightseers, something of the outside world comes with them; and modernism has other more subtle avenues of approach. The cheap daily paper penetrates to these solitudes, and brings with it other things that are cheap. It may leave its readers still credulous and still ignorant; but the nature of the ignorance and the credulity have altered—and perhaps not wholly for the better. There is loss as well as gain. The old traditions have passed from the minds of the people to the guidebooks. Pixies and wish-hounds and spells are now usually only mentioned in jest where they were formerly whispered of in grim earnest. But the beauty of the moorland changes not, and it is its beauty that is our real concern. We can spare the traditions while the loveliness remains.